C000166082

Freshwater Coral Fish

MALAWI

Erwin Schraml

Photos by Erwin Schraml, if not otherwise mentioned.

We would like to thank the following specialists, companies, breeders and hobbyists for their advice and kindly letting us use their slides. We also thank all those we might have forgotten.

Dr. Andreas Spreinat, Ad Konings, Dr. Wolfgang Staeck, Walter Deproost, Christian Wyrich, Manfred K. Meyer, Dr. Lothar Seegers, Hidenori Nakano, Don S. Johnson, Dr. Jay R. Stauffer, jr., Burkhard Migge, Frank Teigler

Aquarium Glaser GmbH,
for providing beautiful fish for our photographers
from their weekly imports

amtra - Aquaristik GmbH,
for providing furnished aquaria
and equipment for testing

Veterinary consultant:
Dr. med. vet. Markus Biffar,
veterinarian, fish specialist

Further useful tips about care and maintenance can be found every six weeks in AQUALOGnews, the unique newspaper for all friends of the hobby.

Read, for example, the latest breeding reports in the news. It is available in German or English and can be obtained at your local pet shop or subscribed to at the publisher.

Order your free specimen copy!

More information about literature you will find at the end of this book on pages 37 and 46.

Die Deutsche Bibliothek - CIP-Einheitsaufnahme

AQUALOG: *Special* – Serie Ratgeber
Mörfelden-Walldorf: A.C.S.
CORAL FISHES FROM FRESH WATER – MALAWI - 1998

CORAL FISHES FROM FRESH WATER – MALAWI
Erwin Schraml

ISBN 3 - 931702 - 49 - 9
NE: Schraml, Erwin

© Copyright by: Verlag A.C.S. GmbH
                   Rothwiesenring 5
                   D-64546 Mörfelden-Walldorf
                   Germany

Author:
Erwin Schraml
Scientific consultant:
Dr. Andreas Spreinat
Dipl. Biol. Frank Schäfer
Translation:
Mary Bailey
Index and organisation:
Wolfgang Glaser
Editor:
Dipl. Biol. Frank Schäfer
Cover Layout:
Gabriele Geiß, Büro für Grafik, Frankfurt a.M.

Print, typesetting, processing:
Lithographics: Frank Teigler/Verlag A.C.S.
Prepress/Photo processing/Layout: Bettina Kirsch

Print: Giese-Druck, Offenbach
Printed on EURO ART,
100 % chlorine free paper

Editors adress:
Verlag A.C.S. GmbH
Liebigstraße 1
D-63110 Rodgau
Phone: +49 (0) 6106 – 64 46 91
Fax: +49 (0) 6106 – 64 46 92
E-mail: acs@aqualog.de
http://www.aqualog.de

PRINTED IN GERMANY

Cover Photos:
A81510 *Sciaenochromis fryeri* – E. Schraml
A39913 *Labidochromis caeruleus* „Yellow" – E. Schraml
A05859 *Aulonocara baenschi* „Orange" – E. Schraml
pp 2/3: Rocky bay, Lake Malawi – Dr. W. Staeck

Acknowledgements

All those who have supported me during my years as an aquarist and fish-photographer have helped bring this book into being, and I owe them a debt of gratitude.

Rudolf Dunz, who showed me how to become a serious aquarist; Georg Wildenauer, who was always happy to let me take photos in his shop during my early years as a fish photographer; Hans J. Mayland, the first to show an interest in my photos; Walter Deproost and his wife Chris, who for many years have made me at home during my visits to Belgium and Holland on aquaristic business. Not forgetting other friends from various organisations, even though I cannot mention them individually here.

Directly involved in this book were Dr. Andreas Spreinat and Dr. Wolfgang Staeck, who provided additional photos; Ralf Paul, who supplied additional information on the treatment of sick fishes; Frank Schäfer who not only supplied technical advice on the software used in the writing of the book, but was also a source of helpful discussion on taxonomic matters; and last but not least, Ulrich Glaser senior, for his confidence in my ability to write this book.

I would also like to thank my wife Brigitte for allowing me the time necessary to write this book.

Augsburg, June 1998.

Contents

About the author

Erwin Schraml

Erwin Schraml was born in Augsburg in 1957. At a relatively early age he developed a keen interest in the fishes of his native land, with the element of mystery a particular attraction; fishes elude normal observation methods by virtue of their quite different environment. Armed with net, rubber boots, and a bucket he wandered along drainage ditches and the local canal, drained for a short while for cleaning. In the case of the latter, every year he rescued many fishes from death by suffocation in the residual puddles; the larger specimens were transferred to the nearby river, but small ones were often taken home for further study, mainly in the wash tub. This led to many a scolding from his mother come washday, when she wanted to use it herself! His most ardent wish, for an aquarium, was not granted until he was 13. Naturally the glass container offered a quite different view of his subjects – the fish could now be watched from the side, not just from above. He was also fascinated by the 3-dimensional effect that could be created by the clever use of decor. It was not long before a second aquarium followed, then a third. Before long everyavailable inch of space in the house was occupied by a small piece of underwater habitat. He was occasionally able to earn fishes and food by doing small jobs for a local petshop owner. Eventually his enthusiasm came to the notice of the committee of an aquarium society, who invited him to one of their meetings. And for the first time he met other people (almost) as "fish-crazy" as himself. After a while he became possessed of the urge to share his observations with others, and he gave his first lecture to his club at the age of 15. A year later he joined the DCG (the German Cichlid Association), and after another year his first article for the association was published.

Cichlids were his first great passion. And before long it was no longer enough to describe his observations in words, he wanted to record them with photos as well. First with borrowed equipment, later with an old Practica "Super TL", which had only a manual shutter but was at least a single-lens-reflex camera. This produced the first usable transparencies, which were actually good enough to be published in aquarium magazines. Fishes and fish photography were now the be-all and end-all of his existence. At an aquarium centre in Munich he found just the selection of exotic fishes he was looking for, and this formed the basis of a collection of photos that now numbers thousands and now allows him to contribute to the illustration of numerous books and magazines. Because published information on fishes is easily forgotten and often difficult to find again, he has developed his own data banks in order to catalogue and archive aquaristic and ichthyological information, thus making it easy to access at any time. As an amateur diver he has observed the behaviour of fishes in their natural habitat, thus filling the gaps in his knowledge. Only recently has he been able to undertake journeys to distant places, now that his children are older. Top of his wish-list were Tunisia and the desert mouthbrooders of its oases, as well as Uganda and Lake Victoria, and he has now visited both.

Contact with ichthyologists has helped him to find answers to taxonomic problems. Links with ornamental fish importers have maintained a continuous stream of new species to photograph. Fish have become a major part of his life. He has nevertheless for years managed to pursue a parallel career as a social worker in order to support himself and his family.

Wolfgang Glaser

Foreword

Why write a book on Malawi cichlids, a topic that has already been covered by numerous other authors? Quite simply because there is at present no existing book that says exactly what I want to say.

I have tried to assemble in this book such information as I have myself read over the years and which has triggered an "aha" response. There is also much that I have learned from experienced aquarists and breeders of ornamental fishes. Plus, of course, many of my own experiences have found their way into the text, as Malawi cichlids are also among my own personal "dream fishes", in the most literal sense of the phrase.

This book is directed primarily towards aquarists who have so far had little experience with Malawi cichlids. All the steps necessary for the successful maintenance of these fishes are included. I hope thereby to prevent many beginners' errors and thus save the lives of a few fishes. Perhaps this book will also help avoid the sort of disasters that all too often cause aquarists to "throw in the towel" prematurely, in sheer frustration. In addition a certain amount of interesting background information on the fishes is included. And I am sure that some experienced keepers of Malawi cichlids will, in glancing through the book, learn something new, something they did not know before.

In order to avoid spoiling the flow of the text, I have refrained from crediting every quoted source as I go along; in any case many of the data are now "general knowledge" among keepers of Malawi cichlids, such that it is often quite impossible to say who first put forward a hypothesis or made a discovery.

The terms "Malawi cichlids" and "Lake Malawi cichlids" are used interchangeably, although strictly speaking "Malawi cichlids" also includes those cichlids that are not necessarily found in Lake Malawi itself, but elsewhere in the territory of the Republic of Malawi. I have, however, tried to avoid this and similar "nit-picking". This book can provide but a glimpse of the immense, impossible to summarise, multiplicity of species that Lake Malawi has to offer, and hence I would like to refer the reader to the two-volume AQUALOG pictorial catalogue, which for the first time illustrates all the known species from Lake Malawi, with colour photographs.

I have also tried as far as possible to avoid the use of scientific terminology, while those terms that are printed in shadowed type in the text are explained in the glossary. The Lake Malawi aquarist must, however, familiarise himself to some extent with the Latin names of the fishes, as the majority have no common name and even the trade uses Latin or English names. Those who have difficulty with scientific names may find it some consolation that their pronunciation is unimportant. If a German uses these names they sound German, if a Frenchman uses them they sound French. There is no reason why they should not also sound English!

Malawi Cichlids are the trendsetters of a new type of aquarium hobby. While before the 1970s many aquarium societies regarded cichlid-keeping as virtually taboo, as those aquarists who tried it apparently left the design of the aquarium to the fishes (cichlids were at that time regarded as notorious diggers), Malawi cichlids gradually gave rise to a new way of thinking. The fishes were colourful, as a rule didn't dig, and, being expensive, gave their owner a certain status. It was also Malawi and Tanganyika cichlids that brought large aquaria into fashion. The hobby was given an impetus which removed it from the "home-grown" sphere and made it of economic interest to manufacturing companies, because aquarists who were prepared to spend a lot of money on fish were more inclined to delve deeper in their pockets for technical equipment. Thus the hobby became what it is today, and Malawi cichlids played a part in its evolution.

Erwin Schraml

General
Introduction

What are the reasons for installing an aquarium in the home? As a rule the tank, the equipment, and the fishes, cost a lot of money. Ongoing maintenance involves additional expense, as electricity is required for heating, lighting, and pumps, moreover there is food to be paid for. But people like to keep creatures from quite different environments to their own – and this applies to most other domestic pets as well.

A lot of preparatory effort is required for these creatures – one must read up on them in the literature and acquire the knowledge necessary to keep them properly.

One must devote lots of time to the new hobby, possibly at the expense of other activities. First the aquarium must be set up, and then it must be regularly maintained, likewise the filter. Partial water changes must be made on a regular basis, and the fishes sometimes need to be fed several times each day.

At the same time one cannot cuddle or stroke fishes. So why go to all this trouble and expense? One good reason is to have a little piece of Nature in one's home! Plants and animals thriving in the living-room! A relaxing peaceful atmosphere, and, in addition, a display offering hours of interesting viewing.

There can be few hobbies in which it is possible so readily to find a link between a pastime pure and simple and scientific research. But many behavioural research data have been obtained via aquarium observations. The aquarium makes it possible to learn facts about living creatures which have yet to be published in any book. Many species of fishes which are maintained in aquaria remain quite unknown to science – this includes many cichlids from Lake Malawi.

Science is that which creates knowledge. If we examine the matter more closely, however, we find that for every assertion made by researchers there is a rebuttal by other scientists. The age of Lake Malawi is a case in point: some experts consider it to be 10 times as old as others; likewise the function of eggspots or the significance of the blotched colour morphs. In the final ana-lysis it is all a matter of opinion, and we shouldn't waste our time getting involved in other people's disputes.

Malawi cichlids in particular exhibit an abundance of interesting behaviour. They create territories, defend these against conspecifics and other fishes, display, and spawn. They protect their eggs in the mouth of the female, and sometimes guard their fry for a while after release.

The maintenance of these fish is relatively easy, and their colours are just as bright as those of marine coral fishes, which are far more difficult to keep. Tankbreds are plentiful, so it is no longer necessary to take large numbers from the wild.

The aquarium hobby is a modern and interesting pastime, which thrives on the exchange of ideas and experiences with other aquarists, and to this end it is possible to join one of the many aquarium clubs or specialist cichlid organisations that exist all over the world.

Back in the 19th century, in the early days of the hobby, everything has to be improvised. Nowadays the trade offers practically everything needed for the successful running of an aquarium. Those with no inclination towards do-it-yourself must resign themselves to paying the market price, but many others will perhaps think of ways in which the implementation of the basic principles can be improved. Thus even today, despite all the manufactured products available, the hobby offers abundant possibilities for customising your aquarium. In the first instance, however, it makes sense to stick to what is tried and tested.

If one asks three people for advice, then it may well happen that one receives three different opinions. This book too offers advice, and this may not necessarily be the same as you will receive from other sources. But the advice contained herein has been tested and proven: an aquarium can be run in the manner described in this book without danger of "shipwreck"!

History and Geography
When the first Malawi cichlids were discovered

**The scientific discovery
of Lake Malawi cichlids**

The first cichlids from Lake Malawi were described as long ago as 1864 by the ichthyologist GÜNTHER. At that time part of the lake belonged to the British Empire, and for decades the British Museum (Natural History) was the only institution involved in the description of cichlids from the lake. Likewise GÜNTHER's successors (BOULENGER, REGAN, TREWAVAS) alone had this privilege, with the sole exception of a single collection made by FÜLLEBORN just before the turn of the century, in Tanzania, which at that time belonged to Germany. Some of these fishes were described by AHL, but the larger part of the collection vanished into obscurity. In the 1950s, FRYER and ILES at last expounded ecological aspects of Malawi cichlids in a number of scientific papers. The end of the 1950's saw the start of the aquaristic discovery of the cichlids, a process that continues to the present day. During the ensuing years many cichlids have been described by scientifically experienced aquarists – one has only to think of JOHNSON, KONINGS, or STAECK . Other aquarists have contented themselves with diving in Lake Malawi and making their observations and photographs available to interested aquarists in books and magazines. Nowadays Malawi cichlids are among the best known cichlid species in the world, and the number of species is now estimated as up to 1,500.

**The aquaristic discovery
of Lake Malawi cichlids**

According to STERBA the first importations of *Melanochromis auratus* took place in 1958. Elsewhere it is stated that Davies was responsible, sending a small sample consignment to a Hamburg importer (Griem) in 1964. Shortly afterwards the first catching station was established at Cape Maclear. Soon afterwards Aquarium Hamburg received regular supplies of fishes, at first *Melanochromis auratus* (at that time still included in *Pseudotropheus*), *Labeotropheus trewavasae,* and *Maylandia* (at that time also *Pseudotropheus*) *zebra.* Further species from the mbuna group followed shortly thereafter. The first breeding report (on *M. auratus*) was published by CHLUPATY in DATZ in 1965,

and in the same issue LADIGES discussed the species thus far imported from the lake. Then things went rather quiet again. This may have been as a result of the high prices that, of necessity, were charged for wild-caught specimens. Not until 1972, when a travel report by STOLZ appeared in TI-Informationen, did the aquarium maintenance of Malawi cichlids become more popular in the hobby. The fact that Cichlid Associations were founded in 1970 may also have had something to do with it. Exchange groups were soon organised and tankbreds were at last available at affordable prices. The first non-mbuna, e.g. *Cyrtocara moorii, Nimbochromis venustus,* and *Copadichromis species* (all at that time included in *Haplochromis*) were soon being imported. There were by now several exporters. In 1973 Stuart Grant began to despatch fishes and soon had a monopoly on exportation from the Malawian part of the lake. The civil war in Mozambique meant that fish collecting was possible there for only a short time. The poor infrastructure in the Tanzanian region reinforced the Malawian monopoly for a long time. It is only in recent years that this has changed, such that nowadays we can obtain fishes from all three countries bor dering the lake.

**Lake Malawi (or Lake Nyasa),
the home of Lake Malawi cichlids**

Lake Malawi is also known as the "warm heart of Africa". It lies south of the Equator, between latitudes 9°30' and 14°25', and roughly between the 33rd and 35th lines of longitude. The major part of teh lake (about 800 km of coastline) lies in the territory of the republic of Malawi, which has given the lake the name most commonly used today. During the colonial period (until 1964) the lake was part of the British Empire and known as Lake Nyassa, and for this reason the region was likewise for a long time known as Nyassaland, and the first cichlids came to us as Nyassa cichlids. In the Tanzanian territory (the north-east part of the lake) the old name is still current. Until the beginning of the 1990s the infrastructure of that country didn't permit the organisation of commercial exportations from the Tanzanian area, which encompasses about 300 km of the lake shore.

History and Geography
When the first Malawi cichlids were discovered

The third country adjoining the lake, in the east is Mozambique, with the shortest section of shoreline (about 200 km). For many years Mozambique was a Portugese colony. Civil war raged in this country for more than 20 years, and in consequence during that period no fishes could be caught for the ornamental fish export trade in its territory.

Today Malawi cichlids are exported in large numbers from Mbeya in Tanzania by the company LANYAFI, and, of course, Stuart Grant, at Salima in Malawi, still plays a significant part in the aquarium distribution of these splendid fishes. His fishermen were also the first to make collecting trips to the Mozambique shore when this once again became possible. Grant has also for many years collected fishes from the large Malawian islands of Likoma and Chisumulu. He is now breeding large quantities of the most popular species.

Other well-known collection sites are the Mbenji and Kande islands, Nkhata Bay, Lions Cove, Jalo and Taiwan reefs. If one looks at a map of Lake Malawi, then it is immediately apparent that many of the names shown there have a familiar ring.

Even the names of places that now lie in the Lake Malawi National Park, from which fishes can no longer be caught for the ornamental trade, have not yet passed into oblivion. Peter Davies had his first collecting station near Cape Maclear (now in the middle of the National Park). Monkey Bay, the Maleris, the islands of Thumbi (East and West), Boadzulu, Chinyankwazi, and Chinyamwezi, are all still famous as the collection sites for fantastically beautiful cichlids. Although Lake Malawi is up to 700 metres deep, only the upper 200 or so metres are habitable by fishes. In contrast to Lake Tanganyika, however, no deep-water cichlids are caught for export, so that the deep-water fish fauna remains largely unknown. The sole outflow from Lake Malawi, the Upper Shire River, lies at the southern end of the lake, and flows south

Biotope
Where do these fishes come from?

left: Male Melano-
chromis johanni,
a typical mbuna
(**A43920**).

right: Protomelas
"Mbenji Thick Lip", an
example of a rock-
dwelling non-mbuna
(**A30165**).

into nearby Lake Malombe, where particularly large specimens of *Cyrtocara moorii*, the Malawi Blue Dolphin, have been caught. Lake Malombe is very shallow (only about 4 metres deep), and in the last century, during a low-water period, dried up completely so that only a small channel was left.

At its southern end the Shire River bears the lake water away to the Zambezi, which in turn carries it down to the Indian Ocean.

Lake Malawi has a few affluents, the largest being the Ruhuhu River. Fishes from this river are not, however, caught for the aquarium trade.

CICHLID BIOTOPES IN LAKE MALAWI

Five different types of biotope are recognised from Lake Malawi, together with the transition zones between them.

The rocky coast

By rocky biotopes we chiefly understand the upper, light-permeated, areas which are inhabited mainly by mbuna. This group of fish includes members of the genera *Cynotilapia, Labeotropheus, Labidochromis, Petrotilapia, Melanochromis, Maylandia* and *Pseudotropheus*. Almost all of these fishes live on the Aufwuchs, the different types of threadlike algae and the various organisms living among them, e.g. insect larvae and crustaceans. Of course this biotope also contains fishes which live on other fishes or parts of them.

High population densities and species variety are characteristic, with both decreasing significantly at depths of more than 20 metres, although the same species

*Aulonocara jacobfrei-
bergi "Eureka", an
example of a cave-
dwelling cichlid from
somewhat deeper
regions (**A05901**).*

*Aulonocara baenschi,
another representative
of the deeper-water
cave-dwelling
"peacocks" (**A05855**).*

Where do these fishes come from?

can be found as far down as the light penetrates and hence algae grow, i.e. to about 40 metres.

The transition region between the rocky coast and the deep water zone is a region of caves and grottos, which have their own special cichlid fauna. Here we find many representatives of the genera *Aulonocara* and *Otopharynx,* but also *Pseudotropheus.*

There is also a transition zone between rocky littoral and sandy bottom, typified by isolated piles of rock or scatterings of boulders and stones. This area is home to cichlids belonging to quite separate groups of *Aulonocara* and *Pseudotropheus,* as well as *Copadichromis* species.

The transition zone between rocky shore and open water is inhabited by certain *Copadichromis* species in particular, i.e. those belonging to the so-called Utaka group. There are also a number of predatory cichlids here, for example *Champsochromis, Dimidiochromis,* and *Tyrannochromis.*

The sandy bottom

The sandy bottom must also be subdivided into various categories. The first of these is areas where light penetrates to the bottom, which is covered in part with beds of *Vallisneria* or may be lined with reeds in the shore zone. Or may be simply bare open sand.

These three habitats are occupied by different cichlids which are specialised to fit their surroundings and adapted to particular ecological niches. Over the open sand one can find *Lethrinops, Fossorochromis,* and *Cyrtocara;* the *Vallisneria* beds are home to *Cyathochromis* and *Hemitilapia;* while *Dimidochromis compressiceps* and members of the tilapiine group are typical of the reeds. The second major category of sandy bottom is

The deep-water zone

Although Lake Malawi is up to about 700 metres deep, fishes can penetrate only to about 200 metres, as below that level there is no dissolved oxygen. The habitable

deep-water zone has been only poorly studied. Cichlids, for example members of the genus *Alticorpus,* have been caught there by trawl. This zone merges into the next biotope

The open water

Only in the past few years have researches shown that there are also typically pelagic cichlids in Lake Malawi, which feed mainly on copepods (small crustaceans). These are members of the genus *Diplotaxodon,* and the genus includes not just crustacean-feeders but also the piscivores of this biotope. A number of new species, previously totally unknown to science, have been described very recently. Some have even been imported for the aquarium hobby.

River mouths

are the fifth and last category of biotope with their own groups of species. Here we find, for example, *Pseudocrenilabrus, Tilapia, Oreochromis,* and *Serranochromis.* Many other, non-cichlid, species are also known from the river mouths, including the characin *Alestes imberi* and various mormyrids (Mormyridae).

A little evolutionary history, anatomy, and systematics

Malawi cichlids are members of the extremely successful perciform (perch-like) fishes, one of the most highly evolved groups of teleost (bony) fishes. In evolutionary terms they are fairly recent; the first fossil perciforms are found in beds dating from after the Cretaceous (which ended about 65 million years ago). The first fossil cichlid dates from the old-world Oligocene (about 26 million years ago). But it is unlikely that cichlids are indeed so recent, as they are nowadays found in America, Africa, and Asia, and thus it must be assumed that they originated in western Gondwanaland, the western prehistoric continent, which was, however, already drifting apart towards the end of the Cretaceous.

On the other hand it may be that phylogenetically similar, marine, ancestors of the cichlids colonised freshwaters twice, in

Evolution
Anatomy and place in the zoological system

Africa and South America. Numerous Madagascan cichlids are more closely related to the Indian species than to those of continental Africa. The reason for this is that Madagascar, like India, separated from Africa at a very early stage. Thus the cichlids found there are very old forms.

Lake Malawi is part of the East African rift valley system and itself probably owes its existence to plate tectonics. Its age is estimated at between 1.5 and 20 million years. Although there have been variations in its water level, affluents, and outflows, it has been filled with fresh water for at least 1.5 million years. Plenty of time for cichlids to adapt to fill every ecological niche.

Cichlids are secondary freshwater fishes – their ancestors were sea-dwellers. Systematically speaking they belong to the suborder Labroidei (wrasse-like fishes). It has been argued that this ancestry has permitted cichlids easily to acclimatise themselves to lakes with a high pH, but this viewpoint ignores the fact that cichlids have also managed to adapt to extremely mineral-poor water (one has only to think of the discus or the fluviatile species of the Congo).

In Lake Malawi two different cichlid lineages (evolutionary lines) are to be found, the tilapiine and the haplochromine. While the tilapias have evolved only an insignificant number of species, the haplochromines have undergone "explosive" speciation, and today there are probably more than 1.500 species, occupying practically every imagineable ecological niche.

Some scientists consider that the reasons for this evolutionary success lie in the cranial morphology (skull structure) of the fishes. Cichlids have two different sets of teeth; first there are the maxillary (jaw) teeth, which can often clearly be seen with the naked eye and which are adapted to the various foods available. The teeth, which are sometimes individually mobile, and have "crowns" of various forms, are set in one or more rows in both the upper and lower jaws, and they are the tools the fishes use to seize, scrape off, or "winkle out" its food.

The second set of teeth are found on a triangular bone in the gullet and are used to process the food. The two sets of teeth can be moved using independently-operating sets of muscles. As a result the food can be broken up before it enters the stomach and intestine, and cichlids are thus able to make better use of their food than fishes that have to swallow it whole, and can thus make use of less nutritious foods.

Interestingly the form of the dentition may itself alter during the development of the individual fish and is thus not entirely genetic. It is known that the molariform pharyngeal teeth of some snail-eaters develop only if, during the process ontogeny, snail-shells are available to crack open. In the absence of snails a generalised dentition develops, similar to that of many insectivores.

Even the most highly specialised cichlids are able, despite their specialisations, to take advantage of any seasonal glut of food (e.g. a plankton bloom). This means that in the aquarium it is possible to feed all Malawi cichlids on whatever artificial or frozen food is available. There are no obligatory trophic specialists among these fishes.

Now, the fact that all cichlids have these anatomical peculiarities and thus the flexibility to vary their food source, explains their evolutionary success in Lake Malawi vis-a-vis other fish groups, but it does not explain why the haplochromines have speciated so dramatically compared to the tilapiines. Some scientists believe that sexual selection is responsible for this.

DARWIN himself recognised that sexual as well as natural selection was a contributory factor in evolutionary change. Sexual selection in haplochromine Malawi cichlids is the prerogative of the female, i.e. in the wild the female selects the males with which she wishes to spawn. The males, meanwhile, endeavour to attract the attention of females by exhibiting the brightest coloration possible and by courtship display.

If the females react especially strongly to a particular signal, then that male will father a particularly large number of fry.

left: Copadichromis azureus inhabits the transition zone between rocky and sandy shore (A25310).

right: Tramitichromis "Lituris Yellow", an inhabitant of the sandy bottom (A95011).

left: Copadichromis verduyni, an example of a fish of the transition zone between rocky reefs and open water (A25400).

right: Copadichromis cf. virginalis, a typical Utaka, which lives in open water near rocks (A25405).

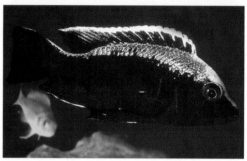

If the courtship behaviour and the female response are genetically fixed, then the offspring of the pair would exhibit both. Thus any change in the components of courtship would very rapidly affect the direct descendants, such that they would differ from other members of their species and, quite simply, no longer be recognised as potential spawning partners.

In addition the process is accelerated by the fact that haplochromine cichlids do not form a pair bond. Thus a new characteristic can spread more quickly throughout the gene pool. This distinguishes haplochromine cichlids from the tilapias.

So far this all sounds very plausible. Unfortunately, however, the genus *Oreochromis* is part of the tilapiine lineage, and just like haplochromines, *Oreochromis* are maternal mouthbrooders that do not form a pair bond.

So why is this genus represented in Lake Malawi by just three to four species,

In the course of evolution the most diverse cichlids have evolved in Lake Malawi. The photo shows Aulonocara stuartgranti "Usisya" (A05949).

Evolution
Anatomy and place in the zoological system

Champsochromis caeru-leus, the "trout cichlid" **(A18670).**

Maylandia sp. "Mbamba Bay Kompact" **(A78540).**

Otopharynx lithobates **(A51890).**

and why has it too not undergone explosive speciation? Likewise how come haplochromine cichlids are represented by several hundred species in Lake Victoria, but not, however, in Lake Tanganyika (although there are some there)? Why the difference between the two great lakes (Malawi and Tanganyika)?

Even the scientists are forced to admit that there is no satisfactory explanation for the situation. Thus further research on Malawi cichlids offers some exciting prospects in this respect.

THE RIGHT WATER
FOR MALAWI CICHLIDS

The water of Lake Malawi

Lake Malawi is one of the largest freshwater lakes on Earth. Because of its immense volume the composition of its water is extremely stable and does not undergo any significant variations.

This also applies to the tropical temperature of the surface layer (between about 26 and 30 °C) and the lack of any deep-water currents to cause any appreciable degree of mixing of water layers with different parameters. The geology of the surrounding area has given Lake Malawi an alkaline pH of roughly 8–8.5. The carbonate hardness is about 5°KH and the total hardness about 14°DGH. Temperature variations in the upper layer derive from the fact that the water in shallow bays is less readily able to mix with cooler water from the underlying layers.

**The correct water
in the aquarium**

Although the hardness of Lake Malawi is not particularly high, in the hobby it is invariably stated that the fishes are best kept in hard water. This is because hard water has a greater buffering capacity relative to its ion concentration, and thus permits a more stable, alkaline, pH in the aquarium.

While the fishes are tolerant as regards hardness, they are not as accommodating as regards pH, especially if it drops into the acid range. Thus the pH should never be allowed to drop below 7.0 in the aquarium! Most inhabited areas have hard slightly alkaline water which is suitable for Malawi cichlids without any modification. Less fortunate aquarists can buy chemicals to harden their water, from the aquatic trade. This is relatively expensive, when one consi-

ders that large aquaria are obligatory for Malawi cichlids.

The water temperature should be between 24 and 27 °C. It is true that the temperature in the surface waters of Lake Malawi reaches higher temperatures, but these are not necessary for the well-being of the fishes and will push the heating bills unnecessarily high. However, it is good to know that we do not need to implement cooling measures in the height of summer as soon as the 30 degree mark is reached; provided the oxygen supply is adequate the fishes should survive such temperatures.

Nitrite

Fishes in general and Malawi cichlids in particular are extremely sensitive to nitrite in the water. Nitrite is a normal product during the course of the breakdown of organic wastes. Nitrite should not be a problem in mature tanks without too large a population.

In newly set up aquaria or those which have been occupied by fishes for only a few days after a move, nitrite can become a lethal problem and wipe out entire tank populations. For this reason newly set up aquaria should not immediately be used for fishes, and only after the initial maturation period should a few fishes be added, and fed moderately, in order to create a certain amount of waste products and thus encourage the development of the bacteria that break down nitrite. After this initial period all the surfaces in the aquarium and filter should have been colonised by bacteria so that after 4–6 weeks nitrite is no longer likely to be a problem.

Nitrate

These bacteria convert nitrite into nitrate, for which Malawi cichlids have a degree of tolerance. Nevertheless nitrate is a toxic waste product and should not exceed specified levels in the aquarium, at least not in the long term.

The cheapest and easiest way of counteracting the inevitable rise in nitrate levels is to make partial water changes with water

Providing the correct water

The water in Lake Malawi is crystal clear in many places. The photo shows an underwater view of Ndumbi Rocks (Likoma).
(Photo: Dr. A. Spreinat)

low in nitrate. Nitrate treatments designed for non-aquarium use, e.g. those used in washing machines, should not be used for the aquarium, as they replace nitrate with chloride and will cause immediate harm, particularly to plants.

The reduction of nitrate to nitrogen, which then easily escapes the water as a gas, is not possible in the aquarium as the process requires an anaerobic (oxygen-free) environment.

It is, however, possible to create suitable anaerobic areas in large external filters with a very slow turnover rate; what then happens is that the bacteria in the first layers of the filter media use up all the oxygen, and

when it is all gone, extract oxygen from the nitrate until only nitrogen is left. But if there is any free oxygen left then the nitrate may simply be reduced to nitrite, which as we have already seen, is highly toxic to fishes. Unfortunately most aquarists lack an understanding of the chemical processes involved and are insufficiently methodical to achieve effective denitrification.

Vigorous plant growth will remove only limited amounts of nitrate from the system. Plants use nitrate as a fertiliser only when they have a high expenditure. So a regular water change (30–50%) is thus unavoidable, and should be performed weekly, or at least fortnightly. Such water changes will reduce

*One of the first signs of excessive nitrate in the water: frequent yawning (in this case Dimidiochromis compressiceps, **A29450**).*

not only the nitrate but also the concentrations of other harmful compounds and those of dissolved salts.

As most aquarists are primarily interested in their own comfort, the water changing should be made as pleasant a process as possible. Permanent flexible pipeing, with taps to control outflow and refilling, are cheaper than outsize filters. If this is nevertheless too expensive, or domestic circumstances do not permit such a system, then at least try to arrange for the aquarium to have a built-in drain point and that the tap can easily have a hose attached and detached.

THE SUBSTRATE

Oxygen-depleted zones are sometimes present in the aquarium, mainly deep in the substrate. In such cases however it is not the reduction of nitrate that takes place, but the production of sulphur dioxide, a foul-smelling gas that is commonly formed in polluted blackish mud. Another toxin unwelcome in the aquarium. It is impossible to avoid such zones completely, but they should not be allowed to get out of hand. These zones result from particles of waste matter and food infiltrating the substrate, and to avoid this I suggest the use of fine quartz sand rather than gravel. If there are areas in the aquarium, e.g. among plants, where mulm accumulates because the current from the filter fails to reach them, then they should be siphoned clean on a regular basis. In the long term, however, it makes more sense to do away with such areas by diverting the water circulation or re-arranging the decor.

Filtration

Filtration is obligatory for Malawi cichlids. Only with considerable knowledge and suitably-sized aquaria is it possible to risk experiments in keeping these fishes without filtration. The type of filter medium used has more to do with personal views than actual success. The general principle is to sieve large particles out of the water, and to provide a large surface area for beneficial bacteria to colonise. The filter medium should, however, above all be easy of maintenance, for

which reason "sponge" filters alone are used almost exclusively in commercial breeding establishments. How often to clean the filter is once again a matter of opinion. One thing is certain: it is necessary when the filter turnover rate starts to diminish. There are, however, aquarists who like to do this job weekly, and this does no harm.

The filter turnover normally also serves to circulate the water and facilitate the absorbtion of atmospheric oxygen by the water. For this reason the pump operating the filtration should be of a capacity appropriate to the size of the aquarium and its fish population. It is better for the pump to be somewhat more powerful than necessary and its full capacity unused, than too small with no reserve for emergencies.

As far as efficiency is concerned, it makes little difference whether the filter medium is housed in an internal or external filter. External filters with hoses have the advantage that they occupy no space in or next to the aquarium, but can be sited anywhere near the tank (e.g. underneath it).

External filters sited next to the aquarium require shorter hoses and are easily removed for cleaning. Internal filters reduce the useable capacity of the aquarium, but are the easiest in terms of convenience and avoiding leakage.

I do not intend to recommend one system above another – it is up to the individual to make his own choice according to his own ideas and requirements.

Some filter media are totally unsuitable for use in the Malawi cichlid aquarium, e.g. peat, which is useful for acidifying water, but exactly the opposite of what is required in a Malawi tank. Activated carbon is likewise of little use, as although it removes toxins from the water, it is primarily chemical toxins for which it is effective – for example, for the removal of medications after treatment or the purification of contaminated water. Situations which are not normal circumtances in the aquarium. Activated carbon may also remove many trace elements which are useful for fishes and plants.

Setting up the aquarium
Technics, heating, lightning

Supplementary biological filtration

Supplementary biological filtration is a luxury in the Lake Malawi aquarium – regular water changes are, as already explained, a better and cheaper method of maintaining water quality. However, boxes of plants, filled with pellets of laterite such as are sold for hydroculture, can be sited above the aquarium for decorative effect. A separate small centrifugal pump can be used to feed water into the container, from which it simply overflows back into the aquarium. This will provide a miniature biofilter which will reduce the nitrate a little and provide a home outside the aquarium for the type of decorative plants used in hydroculture. Many aquarists swear by this method.

Oxydators

Although oxydators are not generally widespread, they can be of significant assistance in improving the "climate" of the aquarium. Their effect is to neutralise large amounts of toxins more quickly that would otherwise be the case. Manufactured oxydators can be purchased; these have to be filled with 6% hydrogen peroxide solution (use distilled water for dilution!) and are easy to install in the aquarium, where they can easily be concealed behind the decor if thought unattractive to look at. The catalyst in the oxydator has the effect of slowly releasing hydrogen and oxygen radicals from the hydrogen peroxide, the latter forming molecules of free oxygen which escape through a hole in the container into the aquarium, where they combine with, for example, metabolic waste products, which are thus rendered harmless.

Heating

Malawi cichlids are, of course, tropical fishes and, in order to remain healthy, require temperatures which cannot normally be achieved without heating. Nowadays the trade offers reliable heater/thermostats which satisfy all the requirements. Standard heaters are particularly suitable, although they have the disadvantage that the temperature of the water is higher than that of the substrate, which some species of plants do not like. The use of substrate heaters is,

however, difficult on account of the rockpiles commonly used in Malawi tanks. The considerable weight of the rockwork can destroy the wiring in the heater if the rocks are subsequently displaced.

If this method is nevertheless chosen, then for reasons of safety a low voltage heater cable should be used. Heater mats are placed beneath the aquarium and are even safer. But they have the disadvantage of a high rate of heat loss to the surrounding area, especially if the tank has a thick base, even more so if it has a double layer of glass, as is often advised for Malawi tanks for reasons of safety (see page 21, "Decor").

It is not easy to calculate the wattage of heating required. The old rule of one watt per litre is not strictly necessary in centrally heated houses but it is nevertheless a valid formula. It is more energy-effective to heat the water up quickly and then let the heater switch off than to have a low-wattage heater running continuously. Even so $1/2$ watt of heating per litre is adequate in rooms that are constantly well-heated.

Lighting

Malawi tanks which are sited in rooms with windows can be run, if necessary, without artificial lighting. But the aquarium will, of course, look a lot more beautiful with lighting! The trade offers lighting covering all areas of the spectrum, and it is very much a matter of personal taste which type you choose. There has long been much discussion as to which area of the spectrum produces the best growth of plants – and also undesirable algae!

For example, "blue-green algae" is said to grow less well under neutral white light than under daylight white light which contains a smaller red component. But this debate is best left to the experts. It is enough for the normal aquarist to understand that different types of lighting and different photoperiods may influence the growth of plants and algae. Because some types of algae are in fact quite decorative, and also act as a natural resource in the Malawi aquarium, there is ample room here for experimentation.

above: Protomelas sp. "Steveni Taiwan" (A75105).

middle: Protomelas taeniolatus "Red Empress" (A75204).

below: Maylandia lombardoi exhibits its full panoply of colour in the right light (A78480).

injure themselves, for example if the main light is switched on suddenly. It is therefore no bad idea to leave a "moonlight lamp" burning when the main light is switched off. Special blue tubes are available for the purpose in the trade.

Carbon dioxide fertilisation

Carbon dioxide, when dissolved in water, forms dilute carbonic acid and thus has an acidifying effect. This may have harmful side-effects in a Malawi cichlid aquarium, where acidity is undesirable, although the effect is relatively slight where the water is very hard, and CO_2 does have an outstanding fertilising effect on plants. Anyone who likes a decorative aquarium full of greenery is well advised to use carbon dioxide fertilisation, especially where cichlids are present.

Economy tip: use only cylinders with a capacity measured in whole litres, as refills are charged by the full litre. The carbon dioxide fertilisation should always be linked to the photoperiod, as plants can absorb CO_2 only in the presence of light. At night it may cause harmful, sometimes fatal, hypoxia in the fishes, as plants actually give off carbon dioxide in the dark.

THE RIGHT SIZE AQUARIUM

It is necessary to calculate the minimum size tank required, which will depend on the fish species one wishes to keep in it. To be sure it is possible to keep two or three species of mbuna in an 80 litre aquarium, but double that size is too small for one *Fossorochromis rostratus*. Relatively deep aquaria are more impressive than shallower ones, and this applies to the front-to-back width as well. The length of the aquarium should be limited only by the available space.

Nightlights for fishes?

You may be aware that small children are often afraid of the dark, and in consequence special "nightlights" are available to provide a calming twilight illumination in the child's bedroom.

Do fish need something of this sort? Perhaps! It is the case that fishes orient themselves in the dark by means of their lateral line system, but it can happen that cichlids panic when disturbed and may thus

Setting up the aquarium
Decor – stones, roots and more!

If you are going to go to extremes, don't forget the structural integrity of the flat or house! A thousand litres of water weigh a tonne, and there are not a few cases on record of cichlid tanks causing wooden floors to collapse or concrete ones to split.

Nowadays it is easy to make tanks containing thousands of litres of water, and I know several private aquarists who have fulfilled this dream. But this "gigantism" is not essential. I have also seen splendid tanks of Malawi cichlids with a capacity of only 150 or 200 litres.

DECOR FOR THE LAKE MALAWI AQUARIUM

As we have already seen, in nature Malawi cichlids inhabit very different biotopes. For this reason there are no hard and fast rules regarding the decor for an aquarium intended for these fishes.

Stones and rocks

Of course rockywork is a typical component of a Malawi tank. This is the most biotope-correct decoration for most mbuna species. It can, however, be recommended for other species as well, as it is thus possible to provide plenty of hidingplaces for subordinate individuals. Stones and rocks should be built up in the empty aquarium before the substrate is added. Some species of Malawi cichlids dig, and can bring the whole edifice crashing down if they undermine it.

In order to prevent the enormous weight from being transmitted to the bottom glass at points where rocks contact it, it is a good idea to build the rockwork on an "underlay". Thin PVC sheet is ideal, and should be laid directly on the bottom glass over the entire area of the intended rockwork. One must take similar precautions when leaning rocks against the back glass.

When building up the layers of rock there are a few general rules to be observed, for example use the large pieces at the bottom. It is possible to stick the rocks together, e.g. with silicone sealant, but this is not strictly necessary as long as the structure is stable.

The type of rocks used is important. Most may leach minerals into the water. There is no objection to calciferous rocks for Malawi cichlids.

Decorative "lava rock" may contain heavy metals and other compounds that are toxic to fishes. Likewise artificial rocks such as paving stones may release lime which may result in clouding of the water and adverse effects on the health of the fishes. Sharp-edged rocks should likewise be avoided, as, during squabbles or in panic situations, the fishes may swim into them and injure themselves.

Roots used as decoration in the Malawi aquarium (the photo shows A39913, Labidochromis caeruleus "Yellow" in front of a piece of root).

A typical background for a Malawi aquarium – rockwork. The fish in the foreground is Maylandia greshakei (A78415).

Setting up the aquarium
Decor – stones, roots and more!

Roots

Pedants might argue that there are hardly any roots in Lake Malawi and so there is no place for them in aquaria containing these fishes.

Anyone not bothered about such niceties can, nevertheless, use roots, which are in fact a very decorative accoutrement in the creation of our aquarium. However, it is important to remember that even after many years roots may still leach tannins and other substances into the water, turning it a brownish colour, although with regular water changes that is not a problem. All the types of roots sold for the aquarium hobby can be used, e.g. bogwood and mangrove roots.

On the other hand, roots found in the forest, or which have been pulled from the water of a river, may contain so much soluble material that they should not be used for the aquarium.

Artificial materials

Ever since Malawi cichlids first arrived on the scene, aquarists have been experimenting with all sorts of artificial walls of rock for the aquarium. Styrofoam blocks have been melted to shape with bunsen burners and edifices constructed from plastic pipe. Fibreglass, as used in boat construction, has been used to create background "rockeries".

All these artificial materials are reputed to contain chemical compounds which may be toxic to fishes. Anyone with an inclination towards this type of do-it-yourself decor should, for the safety of his fish, first consult with other hobbyists who have previous experience in this field. Aquarium clubs are the place to meet like-minded people for this purpose.

Anyone who finds the whole business too much can instead obtain foam-formed background walls via the trade. Unfortunately high quality products are correspondingly expensive, but they are such perfect simulations of a natural backdrop that even a professional will be unable to distinguish them from the real thing just by looking. In addition artificial backdrops have the advantage of being considerably lighter than real rocks.

PLANTS

Before the advent of Malawi and Tanganyika cichlids led to a real cichlid boom, many aquarists assumed that only plastic plants could be used in cichlid aquaria. Luckily this restriction is not necessary with Malawi cichlids. As we are using hard water as a rule, some plants are, however, unsuitable, because they require softer water in order to thrive. But it is not true that only very robust plants can be used. The majority of Malawi cichlids do not dig, and equally do not eat plant leaves, so the assortment of plants that can be used is not that small.

It is important not to simply add new plants in existing territories, as they will be regarded as a "thorn in the flesh" by the territory-holder(s). It is best to introduce the plants a while before the fishes, so that their roots can take hold and the fishes readily accept them as part of their surroundings.

In the following paragraphs I will catalogue a few plants that are particularly suited to a Malawi tank, even if they originate from totally different geographical areas.

Java fern
(Microsorium pteropus)

Java fern is often used in the Lake Malawi aquarium, although it comes from south-east Asia. It does not need much light and copes readily with hard water. It is particulary good for establishing on the rockwork, as it does not require any substrate in order to grow. It grows from a rhizome which develops clinging roots, and until the fern has attached itself, it should be anchored in place or the rhizome wedged between the rocks. It can also grow emerse.

Java moss
(Vesicularia dubayana)

Java moss is another extremely accommodating plant which can grow into lovely green cushions and which thrives if attached to the bare rocks.

The way of the fish
From lake to aquarium

It is particularly popular for breeding tanks, as the tiny fry can not only hide among the numerous branching shoots but also find all sorts of micro-organisms among the greenery, thereby supplementing their official diet.

Cryptocoryne

A whole series of *Cryptocoryne* species are very well suited for the planting of the Malawi aquarium, for example *Cryptocoryne wendtii,* which adapts well to hard water and reproduces freely via runners. *Cryptocoryne walkeri* requires rather more light than most, and should thus be grown some distance from other plants. It too rapidly carpets the bottom by dint of runners. *Cryptocoryne usteriana* grows quite tall and can be planted in groups. It is particularly suitable for growing in the background and along the edges.

Many other *Cryptocoryne* species are suited to the Malawi aquarium, but, unfortunately, not the delicate types that require soft water.

Aponogeton

Not all *Aponogeton* species can be grown in hard water. *Aponogeton elongatus* can be used, however, provided carbon dioxide fertilisation is employed. This species should be grown singly and given space, and can then grow into a large plant which requires a whole area of the aquarium to itself.

Echinodorus

The swordplants are justifiably popular aquarium plants and some species, e.g. *Echinodorus quadricostatus* are accommodating in their requirements. These plants reproduce rapidly by means of runners, so it is possible to start with just a few specimens. Swordplants will not thrive unless they are given adequate iron.

Vallisneria

Some *Vallisneria* species are native to Lake Malawi. There are a few species that go well in an aquarium of cichlids from the lake. The giant vallis *(Vallisneria gigantea)* is rather difficult, while the smaller species (e.g. *Vallisneria spiralis)* are among the hardiest of aquarium plants. They too require iron. In the event of sudden die-back they should be removed from the aquarium.

Sagittaria

Many members of that genus are excellent and hardy aquarium plants. *Sagittaria subulata* is widespread in the hobby. Many varieties are known. They don´t need too much light, but well illuminated plants grow a lot faster and very dense. *Sagittaria* reproduces by means of runners.

THE WAY OF THE FISH
– FROM LAKE TO AQUARIUM

Many Lake Malawi cichlid species are caught only to order. First the wholesaler tells the exporter what fishes he would like to have as soon as possible. During the regular collecting trips these species can then be caught in the numbers required.

When one considers that all this is taking place in Africa, then one can imagine that organising such an undertaking involves a whole host of logistical and material problems than need to be overcome. Starting with styrofoam boxes and plastic bags and extending to fuel and spares for the boat, plus diving equipment.

The fishes are caught by divers using handnets. One can imagine the skill this requires if one considers just how difficult it is to catch a fish in the limited space of a fully decorated aquarium. In nature the fish has far more opportunity to escape!

The way of the fish
From lake to aquarium

Malawi cichlids and plants are not a contradiction in terms. The photo shows Sciaenochromis fryeri (A81510).

Placidochromis electra (A61105).

When all the fishes ordered have been caught, they are taken back to the export station and kept in a fish-house for a few days until all the species required for the export consignment have been collected together.

Boats are an indispensable form of transport for collecting fishes in Lake Malawi. (Photo: Dr. W. Staeck)

From the export station the fishes, packed ready for air freight, are taken to the airport to continue their journey to another continent. Following completion of customs formalities the importer takes them to his establishment, where they are usually treated with medication, as almost all wild-caught fishes carry parasites.

Transportation stress can cause latent diseases to break out. Only after 2–3 weeks of quarantine are the fishes offered for sale to retailers, who either collect the fishes or have them sent. The fishes may already have been ordered from the retailer by aquarists, otherwise they are kept in tanks in the shop. Because every change of environment may induce the appearance of disease, they are again carefully observed and, if necessary, medicated (e.g. for worms). When buying fishes one should first make sure that they are behaving normally and not lethargic. It is important that they have no injuries, no unnatural black or red markings, no ulcers or obvious diseases such as *Ichthyophthirius* and the like. They should show a fright or nervous reaction to gentle(!) tapping on the glass. If white, thread-like faeces are hanging from the anus, or if the anus is abnormally swollen, then worm infestation should be suspected.

A more accurate diagnosis can be obtained only by examining the faeces under a microscope. If you decide to buy, then the

The way of the fish
From lake to aquarium

One maintenance method: overcrowded mbuna.

fishes should be packed properly. The corners of the bags should be tied or sealed off so that the fishes, which are particularly fond of fleeing into the corners when frightened, do become trapped and isolated from the rest of the water, and thus suffocate. In winter in particular it is important to make sure the water in the bags does not become too chilled. Tropical fishes are very sensitive to large drops in temperature.

Another maintenance possibility: keeping just males.

Once home, the fishes should first be housed in a quarantine tank. The temperature of the water in the bags should be slowly adjusted to that of the tank water. Many aquarists do this by hanging the bags in the aquarium for a while. But this means additional stress for the fishes, which instinctively avoid the water's surface, being genetically programmed to realise that danger from aquatic birds lurks there. Plus they will be "gawped" at from below if there are already other fishes in the tank. It is thus better to place the bag in, for example, a bucket, open it, and gradually fill it with aquarium water.

The quarantine tank should have a sprinkling of gravel, and should have a few hiding-places – roots, caves made of rocks, or similar. The tank should also contain water that matches that of the shop tank, and the filter should already be "run in". Over the next few weeks the fishes should be observed very closely. Are they adapting to their new situation? Are they losing their nervousness? Are they eating and excreting normally? Are they showing any signs of disease?

Only after the fish have undergone these precautionary measures and received a kind of personal clean bill of health, can they be

Sufficient space for each fish.

introduced to the aquarium for which they were purchased. The males should quickly establish territories and start to live a normal "aquarium fish life". The fishes will some become tame, recognise their owner, and come to the front glass when they think they are going to be fed. But, as with a begging dog, they should not be given something every time. Even so it is better to feed them a small amount several times per day rather than one large meal. The worst thing you can do is to feed them heavily several times. As a general rule of thumb, anything not eaten after 5 minutes is too much.

In nature Malawi cichlids spend much many hours each day searching for food, and this food is generally rich in roughage and contains, even in the case of piscivores (think of all the bones!), a lot of indigestible material which leaves the gut in the same state as it arrived via the mouth. In the aquarium it is quite different. Healthy Malawi cichlids are so greedy that at every meal they will try to cram in as much as possible until their bellies are blown up like balloons. And because our artificial foods are rich in proteins and fats, our fishes sometimes become fat, sometimes unhealthily fat. Then they have to go on a diet. This is much easier when it is not feeling hunger gnawing at our ribs, but our fishes. A fast day once a week is highly recommended. Remember, mouthbrooder females manage to survive for 3 weeks without food, so one day won't hurt the fishes. This, of course, does not apply to young fish, which need their daily ration, and tiny fry in particular should not go hungry at all.

If more new fishes are subsequently introduced into the aquarium then bear in mind that almost all Malawi cichlids hold territories (even females in some cases) and that they will have known every occupant of the aquarium personally for some time. The hierarchy is established, a "pecking order" exists. New arrivals disrupt this state of equilibrium and may pose a threat to the "rank" of the long-established fishes, and for this reason they are almost always vehemently chased initially, and have to work hard to establish themselves in the existing hierarchy. In the process the order of rank is almost always altered slightly. At this time both old and new fishes must be watched closely, as it is easy for the initial nipping to result in severe injury to subordinate fishes. If the turmoil persists, it may help to re-arrange the decor, so that all the fishes have to settle in again. Sometimes removing the dominant individual(s) for a while may help.

CHOOSING THE FISH POPULATION

In order to avoid endless conflict among the fishes, the fish population can be planned from the start so as to prevent foreseeable quarrels from arising. There are three methods of doing this.

Firstly one can buy just one male and one or more females of each species, bearing in mind that the various species should be as different from each other as possible and should have the maximum possible diversity of habitat requirements. Specifically this means a few mbuna which will remain in close contact with the rocks, a few Aulonocaras occupying caves, the substrate tenanted by *Lethrinops,* other *Aulonocara,* and/or Malawi shell-dwellers, and the remaining space occupied by a few *Copadichromis, Nimbochromis,* or other former *Haplochromis* species.

The second method is to overpopulate the tank with fishes (about 20 mbuna to 160 litres). This will result in the aggression being shared among the high-ranking fishes so that the subordinate individuals do not have to hide most of the time.

A third method is to keep just males. Aggression levels seem to be higher if females are present. This method, of course, means that the fish will not be able to breed and you will not be able to enjoy observing the courtship and spawning behaviour. You will thus miss out on the most interesting part of keeping Malawi cichlids.

Choosing the fish population
Social behaviour

Intraspecific social behaviour

Just as in coral fishes, the gaudy colours of Malawi cichlid males probably allow them to communicate to conspecifics the information that a territory is occupied, or that here is a potent spawning partner for any female.

At the same time males have the ability, when subordinate, of paling their colours and often taking on coloration in part similar to that of females, in order to signal to dominant individuals that they do not pose a potential threat to ownership of territory.

Nevertheless, in the aquarium subordinate males are repeatedly energetically pursued and harassed, and it is a good idea, if the aquarium is not large enough to allow each male his own territory, to remove the subordinate rivals. Otherwise they have a long "dog's life" ahead of them, despite being fishes!

It is noticeable, particularly among mbuna, that males may behave aggressively towards females if the latter are unwilling to spawn. This is probably connected with the fact that in the lake these fishes occupy permanent territories which they do not leave, even to feed. In the nature, the female only enters the males' territory when she wants to spawn. In the aquarium she is not able to leave his territory. The only food source is the Aufwuchs growing in the territory. A female who approaches the territory but is unwilling to spawn is regarded as a competitor for the food supply. This is probably why females of some species also establish territories, which they defend against other conspecifics .

Those species that are not tied to a territory and those that move from place to place are thus often much more tolerant. This applies to, for example, many Malawian piscivorous cichlids. So the fact that a species has a predatory lifestyle does not mean that it will attack all other fishes in the aquarium. Even so small individuals remain in danger of being regarded as prey. Highly specialised feeders, such as a few scale-eaters, may practise their normal mode of feeding in the aquarium and thus should not be housed with other fishes.

Social behaviour towards other species

Fishes which are neither competitors for food nor rivals for the favours of females can well be housed together in the aquarium. As well as cichlids, Lake Malawi is home to, for example, a few catfishes, barbs, characins, and mormyrids. The fact that most of the Malawian catfishes are large-growing predators rules them out as tankmates. But the Malawi "Syno", *Synodontis njassae*, on the other hand, fits in well with cichlids. In fact *Synodontis* in general are good additional fishes for the Malawi aquarium. If you are not bothered by fishes coming from elsewhere, the the various cuckoo catfishes (*Synodontis multipunctatus* and related forms) can be kept. They will even spawn in association with some Malawi cichlids!

There are also a few species of barbs in Lake Malawi. Because of their shoaling behaviour the form an interesting contrast to the solitary cichlids. Unfortunately they are not often imported and you will probably have to go to a specialist dealer who may be able to order them from a wholesaler. If necessary one can make do with faily large Asian barbs, although this will, of course, be out of keeping with the Malawi theme.

The same principle applies to characins. The authentic Malawi choice range is limited to one species (*Brycinus imberi*) which is rarely imported. But there are several similar species in west Africa (e.g. members of the *Brycinus macrolepidotus* group), which are just as suitable. Even the Congo tetra *(Phenacogramus interruptus)* can be kept with Malawi cichlids without problems.

So far little experimentation has taken place with mormyrids, but it should be equally possible. There are a few species in Lake Malawi, but mainly in the river mouths and reedbeds. They are only rarely captured for the aquarium hobby, but are prized as food fishes by the natives. As far as fishes from outside Lake Malawi are concerned, a few armoured catfishes for example are worth mention.

Diet
Types of food

above: Easier to house together: various non-mbuna.

middle: Synodontis njassae, the Malawi Syno.

below: Barbus trimaculatus.

right: Phenacogrammus interruptus, the Congo tetra, is a suitable tank-mate for the smaller cichlid species.

In particular *Ancistrus* species that have been bred for a long time in captivity and no longer have any specialised water re quirements, can be introduced as scaven- gers. Larger Killifishes *(Epiplatys* and *Aplocheilus)* can occupy the upper levels. As a general rule of thumb, when conducting such experiments the fishes should not be too delicate, should have reached a certain size, and have no inappropriate water requi- rements. Naturally at the same time they should not pose a threat to the Malawi cich- lids (e.g. large predatory characins!). Anyone who does not mind deviating from the Malawi theme will find plenty of scope for experimentation.

DIET AND FEEDING

As already mentioned in the section on ana- tomy of Malawi cichlids, despite their many specialisations cichlids remain able to utilise whatever food is on offer. And they do just that in the wild. Thus Aufwuchs feeders have often been observed snapping up food in a shoal of zooplankton. In Lake Malawi, however, days when such a protein-rich diet is available are the exception rather than the rule.

Dried food

In the aquarium we are offering the fishes this type of rich diet on a daily basis if we use normal dried foods. This generally results in many of our aquarium fishes beco- ming obese. Aufwuchs species should recei- ve a diet rich in green foods. Tablet foods with a high content of Spirulina algae are suited to this purpose. Foods intended for ornamental carp (Koi) contain the same algae and are also well suited to mbuna. Normal flake and cichlid pellets can, of course, be given as well. Within this cate- gory, foods containing a vitamin supple- ment are preferable.

Malawi cichlids are not at all fussy, and can be be easily persuaded to accept practically the entire range of manufactured foods, so they are easy to satisfy.

Dried food has an expiry date, which should always be taken into consideration. In the long term it is best to go for branded pro- ducts, as the manufacturers have used labo- ratory research to develop different types of foods for a huge variety of different fishes.

In general it is best to avoid fish foods that have been developed for the food fish mar- ket (e.g. trout pellets) as such foods are de-

Diet

Types of food

signed to achieve the fastest possible growth rate. And you probably don't want to get your fish to edible size as quickly as possible! A possible exception to this rule is when you are dealing with very large-growing piscivores, such as *Tyrannochromis*, whose appetites are otherwise not so easily satisfied.

Freeze-dried foods are a further alternative, which have a few advantages (apart from the price) and no drawbacks. During the preparation the water content is reduced without losing any nutrient value. It appears that they also retain plenty of taste, as they are greatly enjoyed by the majority of fish species. Because the nutritional value is compressed into a small volume, they can be used very sparingly.

Deep-frozen foods

Frozen foods have become very popular with cichlid-keepers. They are packed in small, sensible-portion, blocks, can be kept for months in the freezer and then defrosted relatively quickly for feeding. They are, however, best kept in the freezer and not in the ice-making compartment of the refrigerator.

It is very important that the food isn't defrosted then re-frozen. It should not be fed frozen, as the cichlids may swallow large chunks and end up with lumps of ice in their stomachs! It is best to thaw the portion of food in a small container of water; it can then be used after about 10 minutes.

Of the available frozen foods, Artemia, Mysis, other small shrimps, and glassworms (white mosquito larvae) are particularly suitable for Malawi cichlids.

Artificial frozen foods

As well as small organisms that are easily frozen, other types of food are also processed in this way.

In the past the chief of these was beef heart with various additives, but after it was subsequently shown that red meat is particularly unsuitable (too rich in fat), instead white meat (turkey, chicken) and fish have

left: Maylandia zebra feeding (A79050).

Petrotilapia chrysos, a typical Aufwuchs-feeder (A56815).

Fossorochromis rostratus feeds on invertebrates which it sifts from the sand (A31950).

Cyrtocara moorii follows sifting fishes and eats anything they stir up from the sand (A28355).

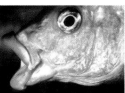

Placidochromis milomo sucks molluscs from rock crannies (A30181).

been preferred as the base material. In addition the flesh of various types of mussels are used, sometimes mixed with spinach, peas, carrots, and other types of vegetables and aromatic spices (e.g. paprika), finely minced, set with gelatine or agar, and frozen in portions. There are meat plants that produce these products specially and supply them to the pet trade.

Live food

Whether live foods are, as often claimed, natural, is questionable. There are gretly differing opinions as to which type of food should be used for which species of fish. Some people maintain that freshwater fishes should not be fed on marine creatures (and vice versa), as the fish is not designed to exploit these foods, while others have had optimum results with them.

The live food most readily available in the trade is Tubifex, which I personally recommend avoiding, as all my failures with Malawi cichlids as a beginner can be attributed to the use of this food. To justify this comment I would add that these worms are found in aquatic substrates that have been heavily contaminated by Man, especially with heavy metals, or so it is generally stated.

On the other hand I would recommend white and black mosquito larvae, as they approximate closely to the natural food of Malawi cichlids. Likewise all aquatic insect larvae are outstanding foods. This also goes for numerous small crustaceans such as water fleas *(Daphnia),* river shrimps, Cyclops, and adult brine shrimp *(Artemia)*. Some of these foods are grouped together under the designation "pond foods".

Ponds were an excellent and cheap source of food for our fishkeeping forefathers, but as far as our generation is concerned, the destruction of wetland biotopes, and regulations regarding the removal of living creatures from the wild, have made things much more difficult. Apropos of which, you should find out what the regulations are regarding the collection of such small creatures in the area where you live.

There are also a large number of other food animals that allow for a welcome variation in the diet of our fishes. However some of them should not be fed on a regular basis. These include whiteworms *(Enchytraeus),* which can easily be cultured at home, but are very rich in fat.

As Malawi cichlids do not absolutely require live foods there is no pressing need to maintain such a culture. Equally unsuitable is food that is too small, unless you are using it as fry food. In nature there are regular periods when certain insects that live near water are present in vast numbers. At such times the majority of fishes live on the innumerable insects that fall into the water. This type of food is likewise, of course, a treat for our fishes. However, whether or not you choose to risk disturbing your domestic bliss by bringing flying insects into the house during the summer months, I will leave up to you!

Hunting for earthworms, of which there are various species, is not everyone's cup of tea, although they are enjoyed by, in particular the larger, Malawi cichlids. After a rainy day it is possible to find large numbers of them on tarmac roads, and they are then easy to collect.

Fry foods

Given proper maintenance, you will probably be unable to avoid Malawi cichlids breeding in your aquarium. As practically all species are mouthbrooders, when the young finally leave their mother's mouth they are already of a size such that they are relatively easy to feed.

Unlike breeders of most other fish species, you will not need to fiddle around with infusorians and micro-cultures. *Artemia nauplii* are the ideal first food for the cichlid fry. The eggs (or, more accurately cysts) of these diminutive saltwater shrimps can survive for years without water, and are available at virtually every aquarium store. In order to hatch them they must be placed in a container of salt water, ideally in a bottle that tapers towards the bottom. The eggs must be constantly circulated using a stream of air bubbles. At a temperature of between

Diet

Specialised feeders

20 and 26°C the nauplii hatch after 24 to 48 hours, and measure less than half a millimetre. They can survive for about 2 days without food.

Once introduced into fresh water these saltwater creatures survive for only about quarter of an hour, by which time they should all have been devoured by the young fishes. For this reason it is important to feed only so many at a time as will actually be eaten, so that the corpses of the excess numbers do not pollute the water of the rearing aquarium.

Anyone for whom providing *Artemia* is too much trouble, will find that the fry of Malawi cichlids can in fact be fed on flake food, which can easily be crumbled to size between the fingers. There are also special, ready-to-use, powdered foods, and slow-dissolving food tablets are not spurned either. Depending on initial appetite, just a quarter of a tablet will suffice for 20-30 fry to start with. Any excess will pollute the water very quickly.

Cyclops, which can be sifted out of "pond foods", are a good food for slightly larger fry, say 1–2 weeks old. However, great care must again be taken not to feed too many of these crustaceans, as Cyclops are able to attach themselves to the skin of fishes and feed there. This can be fatal to delicate young fishes.

Problems with some types of foods

It is as well to mention the various problems that may accompany the use of some types of foods. Live foods, in particular those collected from natural waters, always carry a risk of introducing pathogens. It is especially inadvisable to collect live foods from waters inhabited by fishes. Some waters are so heavily polluted with chemical toxins and heavy metals that food animals should not be collected from them. Unfortunately this applies particularly to water treatment plants – unfortunately, because the latter are a very productive source of live food.

Some authors consider frozen as well as live red mosquito larvae risky, as some species possess bristles which can damage the gut of the fishes, in serious cases even leading to intestinal blockage and hence the death of the fish. I personally have never encountered this problem, but pass on the warning nonetheless.

Many professional breeders have, in consequence, gone over to feeding Malawi cichlids exclusively on artificial foods, and state that these produce the best results. If making your own food, agar agar is preferable as a binder, as gelatine is itself highly nutritious.

Specialised feeders

A number of cichlid species in Lake Malawi have evolved highly specialised feeding habits. We know of species that live on the skin parasites of other fishes (*Pseudotropheus crabro*); egg- and larvae-feeders (*Caprochromis orthognathus*); suck *Vallisneria* leaves clean (*Hemitilapia oxyrhynchus*); eat scales (*Melanochromis lepidiadaptes*); etc. Almost all these fishes, however, can live on quite normal artificial foods in the aquarium.

Today it is generally thought that one species, *Dimidiochromis compressiceps,* the "Malawi Eyebiter", does not in fact eat eyes and that the name is pure fancy. But it appears the matter is not quite that simple after all! However, eye-eating is not an obligatory feeding method, and when sufficient adequate alternative food is provided, this fish does not pose any actual threat to tankmates.

One exception is *Genyochromis mento,* another scale-eater, which refuses to abandon its chosen mode of feeding in the aquarium, and thus cannot be kept together with other fishes.

Although they are commonly referred to simply as "predators", scientists speak of "piscivorous" species. And even those cichlids that feed on other fishes in nature are eminently suited to aquarium maintenance.

Diet
Fish-eating cichlids

Lake Malawi offers a whole selection of species of this type, a few of which are pictured on this page.

Nimbochromis livingstonii, the "sleeper" derives its special name from its behaviour. Its coloration imitates that of a dead, part-rotted, fish, and it lies on its side as if sleeping; this deception is used to try and attract small fishes. If a potential prey item

Observations of *Dimidiochromis strigatus* suggest a large variety of feeding mechanisms – they are said to eat fish, invertebrates, or plants. This species is sometimes seen in the trade as the "Sunset *Haplochromis*", but is rather uncommon although it is distributed throughout Lake Malawi. *Dimidiochromis strigatus* grows to 25 cm in length.

Likewise uncommon, but found along much of the coastline of Lake Malawi, is *Stigmatochromis modestus.* This species has a relatively large mouth but grows to only about 16 cm. It apparently lives solitary in caves, and it is thus sufficient to keep a pair. There must be space enough for the female to hold her own territory.

Dimidiochromis strigatus, the "Sunset Haplochromis" (A29465).

At first glance *Hemitaeniochromis urotaenia* appears to be a typical fish-eater. Males grow to about 25 cm long, and change colour completely when guarding a territory. Although they are normally silver grey (as in the photo) with two lateral bands broken up into individual spots, these markings completely disappear when the fish is in courtship dress. The scales are now instead bluish with red edges.

comes close enough, then the sleeper grabs it suddenly and immediately.

Tyrannochromis macrostoma is fairly common in sediment-rich biotopes in Lake Malawi. It is a very large species, easily growing to 30 cm. These imposing fish also command respect in the aquarium. They should be kept only in larger aquaria with a volume of 300 litres or more.

left: Tyrannochromis macrostoma, a very large predator (A98100).

right: Hemitaeniochromis urotaenia, non-territorial male (A36550).

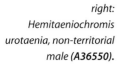

Unusual colour patterns
Polychromatism, OB forms

It is well-known that various species of Malawi cichlids exhibit somewhat different colour patterns depending on where they are found: these are termed geographical variants of a species. All the members of a population have a relatively uniform coloration (minor details aside) – they are not coloured any which way.

Although, in the course of evolution, mutations in coloration do occur from time to time, these are soon expunged, as they are less han optimal for the life requirements of the species in question, because only those colour forms than can find a mate (i.e. that live long enough to be recognised as such by potential partners) get to spawn and thereby pass on the genes for their external appearance. Thus, even when there are several different forms, in the long term it is the most suitable one that survives. For this reason there are very few leucistic or albino

forms in nature – they are mostly so conspicuous as juveniles that predators quickly single them out.

above: Maylandia zebra, OB male, a so-called "Marmalade Cat" (A79099).

left: OB female Maylandia estherae (A78372).

right: OB male Maylandia estherae (A78372).

left: OB female Maylandia estherae, with very few spots (A78372).

right: Completely orange female of Maylandia estherae (A78370).

left: "Red" male M. estherae (A78372).

right: Albino male Pseudotropheus tropheops (A78713).

These two forms are aquarium sports.

Unusual colour patterns
Polychromatism, OB forms

However, an interesting phenomenon occurs in about a dozen species of Malawi cichlids, namely a single population contains a number of different colour forms. This is particularly noteworthy in that the polychromatism is stable, and, in Malawi cichlids, restricted almost exclusively to females, with the different forms always occurring in relatively similar numbers within the population.

Another phenomenon, to date known only from mbuna, is encountered in connection with this polychromatism. The normal colour of females is beige, brown, or grey, sometimes with stripes. The other morph is a striking combination of orange with black blotching, commonly known as "Orange Blotched", hence "OB" morph.

The incidence of the dark blotches is variable, and in consequence there are individuals with very small or no spots, the latter being uniform orange. I can well imagine that the spectrum of the spotting may equally extend in the other direction such that there are uniform blackish-brown individuals. This is certainly the case in Lake Victoria, where polymorphism also occurs. Completely or mainly dark coloured individuals have not been found in the Lake Malawi so far.

Many authors have tried to explain the reasons for the occurrence of polychromatism in Malawi cichlids, but there has been no proper research into the subject. Thus there are several different hypotheses, all as yet unproven.

I myself have formed a hypothesis, which, while not explaining how polychromatic species have evolved, does however offer a plausible explanation of why the blotched and pure orange forms are not rapidly weeded out by selection, although to our eyes they are highly conspicuous. It would appear that the blotched individuals are less striking than we think in their natural surroundings.

It has already been pointed out elsewhere that the spots may represent cryptic coloration, as the rocks are not uniformly coloured but likewise contain sprinklings of dark

colour. Divers are familiar with another phenomenon, and can confirm that colours that are visible in the light present at the surface, disappear more and more the deeper one descends.

At as little as 5 metres of depth red appears as blackish-brown, while below 10 metres orange is no longer recognisable. Yellow can still be seen at 25–30 metres without artificial light. Resorption, as this physical phenomenon is termed, means that in practice the colours disappear; they do not become white, as one might intuitively imagine but are replaced by no colour (i.e. black).

These depth data apply only to relatively clear water, however. In murky water the resorption of colours takes place at shallower depths.

In nature OB females are significantly more orange-coloured as a result of a diet richer in carotene.

Because the types of algae on which mbuna feed are found down to 40 metres, a significant part of their potential habitat lies below the depth at which the orange component of the blotched individuals becomes unrecognisable without artificial light. Their coloration is thus no longer conspicuous. Unfortunately no researches have been conducted into whether OB individuals are proportionally commoner in the deeper part of the habitat occupied by their species.

There are different reasons for the relative paucity of blotched males, the so-called "marmalade cats". Males must be recognisable, to females, as belonging to the same species. They would therefore appear to be at a selection disadvantage if their coloration is inappropriate. Research into the genetic inheritance mechanism by HOLZBERG (1978) explains precisely why the observed distributions take place.

The fact that the particularly striking forms are commonly bred in captivity results from these types, although rarer in nature, being more frequently offered in the trade. This has led to blotched aquarium populations that breed true, e.g. in *M. estherae,* and even some that produce red males.

Diseases
Prevention is better than cure!

Although Malawi cichlids are relatively robust fishes, they do sometimes become ill. Unfortunately some cases of illness result from incorrect maintenance. I have already mentioned that Malawi cichlids require a balanced diet, otherwise their greed may lead to one of the so-called "civilised diseases" – they become far too fat. The best food for these fishes is not that which is most rich in nutrients vis-a-vis volume, and if we are not careful our good intentions may serve only to harm our pets.

The other main preventative measure is regular water changes, lest, despite filtration, the fishes are left swimming in their own wastes. The first sign that the nitrate level is too high is usually excessive yawning by the fishes. It would appear that they experience irritation of the gills, which they try to alleviate by contracting them. Harmful consequences for fish health are likely at a nitrate level of 80–100 mg/l, even though the lethal level (which varies from species to species) may be far higher. Remember that in Germany the law requires that drinking water should have a level no higher than 25 mg/l.

Remaining on the topic of water, all uncoated metals should be kept well away from it. Poisoning by dissolved metals is not uncommon, but is diagnosed only with difficulty. If, for example, your house has copper pipework, then this is a good place to start looking for the cause of any problems of this type, although in hard water areas the insides of the pipes soon become coated with chalk, which seals off the bare copper. Lead, for example that often sold to weigh down plants, also dissolves in water, and should thus not be used.

Correct maintenance, as regards living quarters, is the secret of preventing the third type of harm that may befall our pets. Because the confined space that the aquarium offers does not permit any defeated fish to distance itself from the victor, sufficient hiding-places must be available. If there are not enough, the victor will quickly learn where his rival normally hides, and seek it out there. And in order to avoid a long period of suffering, it is essential to be able to separate off such a persecuted fish.

This may involve using the quarantine tank (which you will, of course, have available). Sharing out aggression by overpopulating the tank has been discussed earlier.

Beginners are advised not to start with wild-caught fishes, at least as their first acquisitions. Tank-breds from responsible breeders are already adapted to aquarium conditions and present fewer difficulties than wild-caught individuals. In addition they will not be carrying any dormant pathogens (e.g. metacercariae).

Another preventative measure for those just beginning the hobby is to avoid live food collected from the wild, as this may harbour the seeds of all types of diseases. Under no circumstances should food be used that has originated from ponds containing fishes. The risk of introducing infectious diseases is too high.

As already mentioned, wild-caught Malawi cichlids will have already been medicated at the wholesaler's to treat any diseases brought on by transportation stress. Nevertheless this does not mean the fish are as healthy as their new owner would like, and it is absolutely essential that new fishes be quarantined in a separate aquarium. The quarantine period can be used not only for observation, but also to rid the fishes of any pathogens they may have picked up in their native waters.

In nature they have to live with a huge variety of parasites for better or for worse, and as a result often do not attain the same age as is possible under good aquarium maintenance. In the long term these parasites weaken the affected fish too greatly, even if it was not particularly bothered by them in its early years. The fishes are able to cope with these parasites only because, after an acute attack, their immune response is able to resist the pathogens and keep their numbers lower.

Recognising diseases in latent forms

Some parasites are so large that they can be recognised with the naked eye. These include, for example, the various fish lice which it is not that uncommon to find on freshly imported fish. If there are not too many of them then the fish can be netted and the parasites simply pulled off using forceps. Take care when handling Malawi cichlids, as even these relatively robust fishes will suffer damage to their skin mucus coating is they are held incorrectly.

If there are too many lice to remove manually, or if the entire aquarium is affected, then chemical therapy may help (e.g. Potassium permanganate) (1g per 100 litres of water,

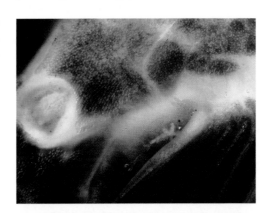

Fish lice may be present singly or in greater numbers

Some tropical fish lice are actually rather attractive under magnification

Cichlid with exophthalmus ("pop-eye"), a problem commonly triggered by poor water quality

for about 90 minutes); Neguvon* (2–3% solution, 10–30 minutes); or Masoten* (2–3% solution for 1–10 minutes).
(*WARNING: Very toxic to humans as well!)

This will also deal with any fish lice living on the gills. In discus in particular it is sometimes possible to remove thumbnail-sized crustaceans from the gills.

Most parasites and other pathogens are, however, so small that they cannot be seen with the naked eye. Sometimes these produce obvious symptoms. This is the case with our old friend *Ichthyophthirius*, often known as "whitespot" or "Ich", a disease still frequently encountered today. Whitespot is very easily transferred from aquarium to aquarium – a net used in an infected aquarium can easily spread the free-swimming stages like wildfire, throughout the entire establishment. Luckily nowadays there are very good medications available in the aquarium trade. Used properly, these can easily eradicate *Ichthyophthirius* from an aquarium. There is also a whole series of other ectoparasites which may parasitise the skin of fishes, but are less commonly seen.

Correct diagnosis of fish diseases is a major problem. Even if advice is sought from more experienced aquarists, the diagnosis is more likely to be wrong than right. In spite of – or because of – this, one should have available one of the various books that deal with fish diseases in aquarium fishes. In the following paragraphs I will, however, draw your attention to a number of methods of treatment which are covered only briefly, if at all, in other publications.

Some pathogens are, at first sight, not as readily identifiable as those that parasitise the skin. Cichlids are prone to a number of intestinal parasites as well. They are tough enough not to die quickly of this problem, but they become unhealthy and give their owner little pleasure, waste away visibly, and may eventually die. But because a number of different parasite groups are involved in intestinal diseases, it is difficult to recommend specific treatments.

Diseases
Treatments for common diseases

Nifurpirinol is effective against many bacterial infections. It is well-tolerated and does not harm aquatic plants. It is readily taken up by the organism and distributed throughout all its organs. It can be dissolved and sprayed onto food tablets (e.g. with a spraygun intended for misting plants). This avoids the need for large amounts of the medication to treat the water in large aquaria.

Non-iodised salt can be used to treat cloudy eyes and fungus, at the rate of 10–15 g per litre for 20 minutes. The fish should be watched closely during treatment. Salt should not be used in planted aquaria. The fish should be treated separately in the quarantine tank.

A few diseases cannot be treated using medications available via the aquarium trade, and if one wishes to save the fish, then the only answer is a visit to the vet or another experienced professional (e.g. a pharmacist who is also an aquarist).

It is absolutely essential to note that any antibiotics used in such cases are also used in human medicine, and that their use can lead to resistance such that if the aquarist himself falls ill, these drugs may prove ineffective.

As these drugs are normally used for serious illnesses in humans, this warning should not be discounted as trivial! One should thus not touch the medication with one's hands or get treated aquarium water on one's bare skin! The instructions on the packet should be followed to the letter! The use of medications which are not freely available should be considered only in serious cases!

If the fishes produce white, threadlike, slimy faeces then intestinal flagellates *(Spironucleus)* must be considered. You will then need to contact a professional and discuss Metronidazole with him.

If this drug is used then a water change of $^2/_3$ of the aquarium volume must be carried out after 3 days, as otherwise serious harm may be caused to the fishes. If the treatment appears to have no effect, then one can try repeating the treatment with Dimetro-nidazole. Experience has shown that some strains of flagellates respond to one but not the other.

If one sees thin appendages protruding from the anus of a stationary fish, then this points to *Camallanus* infestation.

Chloramin-T, at the rate of 1g per 100 litres of water, is effective against skin, gill, and intestinal parasites, nematodes and thread-worms, planarians and *Hydra*.

Literature on fish diseases:

BASLEER, G. (1996):
Colorguide of freshwater fish diseases
distributed by:
Verlag A.C.S., Liebigstr. 1, D-63110 Rodgau

DUNLIN, M. (1979):
Fish Diseases.
T.F.H. -Publ. Inc., New Jersey, U.S.A.

REICHENBACH-KLINKE, H.H. (1970):
Reichenbach-Klinke´s Fish Pathology
T.F.H. -Publ. Inc., New Jersey, U.S.A.

ROBERTS, R. J. (1978):
Fish Pathology
Balliere Tindall, London, U.K.

STOSKOPF, M. (1993):
Fish Medicine
W. B. Saunders W., Pennsylvania, U.S.A.

UNTERGASSER, D. (1989):
Krankheiten der Aquarienfische
Kosmos-Verlag, Stuttgart
(also as T.F.H. book available)

VAN DUIJN, C. JR. (1973):
Diseases of Fishes
London Iliffe Books Ltd., Dorset House, London, U.K.

BREEDING BEHAVOIUR

Almost all the cichlids of Lake Malawi are mouthbrooders, with the female invariably brooding the eggs. Apart from supplying the sperm, the male has nothing to do with the offspring. In parallel with this distribution of labour, in almost all species male and female are quite different in appearance. The males have to make themselves conspicuous by means of their courtship dress, while females commonly exhibit rather plain coloration, as they do not wish to attract potential enemies. Because it is females that seek out males, they do not need to be colourful. In addition males are generally larger and sometimes have striking spots, resembling eggs, on the anal fin. These are in fact intended to imitate the eggs. Because during spawning the females immediately take their eggs into their mouths, nature has had to devise a ruse to get the sperm to where the eggs are. Thus the male spreads his anal fin and displays it to the female so that she thinks she is seeing more eggs and tries to snap them up. At the same time she ingests the sperm that the male is emitting, and in this way the eggs are fertilised in her mouth. Thus, at least, runs the theory propounded by WICKLER as long ago as 1962, and which was accepted for many years.

Much later on, however, other behaviouralists observed that males whose anal fins had been cut off were less successful in attracting females to their nests. HERT (1989), who conducted these researches, concluded that the spots must stimulate females to spawn with males which displayed the anal fin with the spots clearly visible. In addition AXELROD (1973) had already evolved a very similar theory according to which the spots were for recognition purposes, and intended to help females find males in particularly dark corners of rocky crevices.

Now in fact there are a whole series of Malawi cichlids in which the males no longer possess eggspots at all, presumably because they have disappeared in the course of evolution because they were no longer needed. So how is fertilisation ensured in such cases? Probably because spawning behaviour has become so standardised and ritualised over the milennia, and transmitted via the genes,

that the entire process can take place successfully without the lure proferred by the egg-dummies. In these species the female mouths at the anal fin of the male just as if he had eggspots. In some such species is is rather more difficult to tell the species apart, as the males never take on courtship coloration and thus look very much like females.

On the other hand in some species with eggspots there are females that also possess them. In such cases they are almost always fewer in number, and smaller and less visible, than in males. Above all they do not have a transparent ring around the yellow centre.

Sexual differences

A relatively accurate method of telling the sexes apart involves examination of the anal opening, which is smaller in males than in females and differently shaped. This requires a practised eye, and it is advisable to examine a proven pair closely in order to establish what the differences look like. With a little practice then one can sex fish this way when buying them, instead of relying on someone else's opinion.

Breeding

Breeding most Malawi cichlids is simplicity itself. Rumour has it that they have even known to spawn in transit! Then again, it is not always quite as simple as it is made out. A prerequisite is that the male holds a territory, albeit sometimes this is temporary and/or very small. Some species build proper nests, larger than themselves, from sand, while others simply dig a small depression in the substrate; yet others don't bother at all about the appearance of the spawning site, and some spawn in caves. Depending on the species kept, the aquarium should be arranged so as to provide the males with the territorial features they require. Provided this is done, and the fishes are healthy and properly fed, then they will also endeavour to bring offspring into the world.

Some species are willing to mate only seasonally, while others can spawn all year

Breeding
Problem areas

round. Once spawning has taken place (the spawning ritual will be described later), the female withdraws. If we want to save the fry, then we would do well to transfer the female to a separate aquarium. A breeding trap, floating around at the surface, should be regarded as merely an emergency measure.

For most species a mini-aquarium (about 20 cm in length) is adequate for the purpose, fitted with a simple sponge filter and a small heater. It should contain water with the same parameters as those of the aquarium in which the female spawned. It should be decorated with some Java moss and a half flowerpot, so that the female can feel hidden and secure. During the brooding period she will as a rule eat nothing, and should thus not be fed.

The duration of brooding is somewhat temperature-dependent, and in most species lasts about 3 weeks before the fry leave their mother's mouth. By then they will have no yolk sac left and will immediately begin to search for food. In many Malawian species the female practises no further brood care, and can be removed immediately from the container. Species which, when danger threatens, take their fry back into their mouths, can be left with their offspring for a few days longer, although the young will soon be fending for themselves.

Now is the time gradually to begin feeding them. Both mother and fry should be fed only a small amount during the first days, as the water in a small brooding container is easily polluted. It may help somewhat to introduce an apple snail to consume any food residues. Smaller snail species will also do the trick, but we must always ensure that they do not take over, as they themselves can pollute the water with their metabolic waste products.

As a rule further growing on presents no difficulties, as there is no need for any major change in diet as the fry grow on. However the water changing regime will need to be amplified as the young fishes eat more. At some time or other the aquarium will no longer be large enough, and then, if not before, we must transfer the youngsters elsewhere. In the meantime we will probab-

ly have already encountered a different problem – the next female, or maybe the same one again, will have a mouthful of eggs! Thus our little set-up keeps on growing, like it or not, no matter how well-planned to start with.

Problem areas

It sometimes happens that mouthbrooder females turn out to be notorious egg-eaters. Many young females, that have just spawned for the first time, will eat their eggs, because their brood care instincts are not as well-developed as their physiology. If the eggs are again eaten after several spawnings, and we want fry from the fish in question, we can instead "brood" the eggs artificially. First we must take the eggs away from the female. To do this we can fill a large drinking glass almost to the brim with aquarium water. Now we catch the female and hold her between thumb and forefinger with her head in the glass, pressing firmly but gently on the gills to compress them so that the mouth opens. The first eggs will probably fall out straightaway and sink to the bottom. Later, when there are fewer eggs left in the mouth, we can create a slight pumping effect by gently applying and releasing pressure on the gills, thus easily loosening the eggs. Moving the fish to and fro in the glass will also result in the eggs being shaken out. It is important to hold the fish in as vertical a position as possible, with her mouth pointing downwards. The female can withstand this procedure for several minutes without sustaining any damage. Because the eggs have a high oxygen requirement but at the same time their outer casing is delicate, the following method is recommended.

A whisky glass (stable because of its thick heavy bottom, and about the right size) should be placed in the rearing tank with an airline extending into it a little way. The eggs are placed in this glass, trying not to touch them at all with the fingers.

The airline should now be arranged so that the stream of bubbles causes the eggs to vibrate slightly but without whirling them around. Otherwise they might be blown right out of the container, and this might

Astatotilapia calliptera

Hybridisation

Under aquarium conditions Malawi cichlids tend to be less choosy as regards choice of partner than they would be in the wild. This is in part because in the artificial environment barriers are broken down that in nature prevent the intermixing of different species. This may happen if the factors preventing a female from accepting a male of another species as breeding partner are compromised – e.g. because the right mate is lacking, or because two species of very similar appearance, which do not have the opportunity to encounter one another in the wild because they occupy totally different habitats/geographical regions, are kept together in the aquarium.

prevent them from obtaining sufficient oxygen.

Once the larvae are sufficiently well-developed that they can get of the glass "under their own steam", then they will be mobile enough to survive in the aquarium itself. It should be understood that no snails should be present when this method is used, as they may eat the eggs. An alternative method sometimes suggested, using a worm-feeder suspended beneath the filter outlet, is not such a good idea, as the holes in the plastic may be sharp-edged and damage the egg-casings.

According to the definition of a species then two spearate species should, if they cross, prove infertile by the 4th generation at the latest. So far no-one has investigated this in detail as regards Malawi cichlids. And whether or not they continue to the 4th generation, there are unfortunately more than enough hybrids available, produced by irresponsible breeders and purchased by unwary aquarists and spread even further afield. Likewise hybrids are always turning up in the trade; sometimes these are attrac-

left: Labeotropheus trewavasae. Male with clearly delineated eggspots, surrounded by a ring (A39854).

right: Aulonocara maylandi maylandi, a species in which the "eggspots" appear to be purely decorative rather than functional (A05920).

left: Labeotropheus trewavasae, female with eggspots, which are smaller and have no ring (A39850).

right: Aulonocara baenschi "Orange", a species in which the anal spots are missing (A05859).

Breeding
Spawning ritual

The spawning ritual of Malawi cichlids, using Sciaenochromis fryeri (A81510) as example:

The male entices the female to the spawning site …(1)

… and after a few "dummy runs" …(2)

…the first eggs appear. The female turns lightning-fast …(3)

…and picks up the eggs …(4)

…or may swim backwards in order to collect them (5).

Once they are in her mouth she ingests sperm to fertilise them (6).

tively coloured, although they are probably infertile. In the interests of maintaining good quality tankbred stock, hybrids should not be distributed. They can generally be recognised in that the individuals in a brood exhibit a relative variety of patterns.

Spawning sequence

An even more difficult problem is presented by crosses between the different varieties of a species. In such cases there may be no breach in the chain of subsequent generations and with the passage of time different geographical variants become mingled in an appalling mish-mash. We should make every effort to keep species and populations pure, in the interests of keeping all these different fishes in the hobby. If hybrids accidentally occur, then they should never be passed on to anyone else.

The AQUALOG-System
Information and description

AQUALOG Lexicon

The AQUALOG team has set itself the goal to catalogue all known ornamental fishes of the world – and this task will, of course, take several years, as there are over 40,000 fish species.

Compiling an AQUALOG lexicon, we take a certain group of fishes, label all known species with code-numbers, look for the newest results of fish research about natural distribution, features and maintenance of the fishes and try to get the best photographs, often from the most remote parts of the world.

Our ingenious code-number-system labels every species with its own individual code-number which the fish keeps even if a scientific re-naming occurs.

And not only the species gets a number, also each variety, distinguishing locality, colour, and breeding form.

This system makes every fish absolutely distinct for everybody. With it, international communication is very easy, because a simple number crosses almost all language barriers.

This is an advantage not only for dealers, but for hobbyists, too, and thus for all people involved in the aquarium hobby.

Again and again, new fish species are discovered or new varieties bred. Consequently, the number of fishes assigned to a certain group changes constantly and information from available specialist literature is only reliable within certain time limits. Thus, an identification lexicon that is up-to-date today is outdated after as little as one year.

To give aquarists an identification 'tool' that stays up-to-date for many years, we developed our ingenious patented code-number system.

When going to press, our books contain all fishes that are known to that date. All newly discovered or bred species are regularly published as either supplements or as so-called "stickups" in AQUALOGnews.

These supplementary peel-back stickers can be attached to the empty pages in the back of the books.

As you can see, we provide the latest information from specialists for hobbyists. Over the years, your AQUALOG books will 'grow' to a complete encyclopaedia on ornamental fishes, a beautiful lexicon that is never outdated and easy to use.

AQUALOGnews

AQUALOGnews is the first international newspaper for aquarists, published in four-colour print, available in either German or English language and full of the latest news from the aquatic world.

The following rubrics are included:Top Ten, Brand New, Evergreens, Technics, Terraristics, Fish Doctor and Flora. Further, there are travel accounts, breeding reports, stories about new and well-known fish etc.

The news gives us the opportunity to be highly actual, because up to one week before going to press, we can include reports and the 'hottest' available information.

This way, every six weeks a newspaper for friends of the aquarium hobby is published that makes sure to inform you about the latest 'arrivals' waiting for you at your local pet shop.

AQUALOGnews can be subscribed to and contains 40 supplementary stickers for your AQUALOG books in 12 issues. You can subscribe to the news either via your local pet shop or directly at the publishers.

Issues without stickups (print run: 80,000) are available at well-sorted pet shops. The newspaper also informs you about newly published supplements.

AQUALOG Special

The Specials series is not intended to repeat all the things that were already known twenty years ago, like 'how to build your own aquarium' – something, probably nobody practises anymore, because there is no need to do so.

We provide the latest and most important information on fish keeping and tending in precise and easily understandable language.

We want to offer advice that helps you to avoid mistakes – and your fishes to live a healthy life.

We intend to win more and more friends for our beautiful and healthy (because stress-reducing!) hobby.

Order our new free catalogue, where all our previous and future books are shown and described.

*Labidochromis caeruleus „Yellow" (**A39913**)*

*Aulonocara jacobfreibergi „Orange" (**A05902**)*

The future
Recent developments

The first imports from Lake Malawi were sent from the southern part of the lake. Nowadays very large numbers of fishes from the Tanzanian coast are available. New imports have been, and still are, a driving force as regards interest in cichlids; a lot of aquarists seem to think it important to keep fishes about which very little is as yet known, and for these customers Lake Malawi is a real cornucopia of new fishes.

Many species, varieties, and morphs are known but have not been covered in any detail in the literature, so there is a whole field of activity open to those who wish to explore new territory.

And it is as yet impossible to predict when the discovery of new species will come to an end. There are still many areas where no-one has dived as yet, and exploration of deepwater zones is still in its infancy. It is only recently that the first book on the open water zone, with numerous photos of the cichlids found there, has been published. We can also expect as yet unknown species from the slow opening up of the Mozambique coastline. Naturally it is im-

above: Aulonocara sp. „Mamelela" (A05820): according to Ad Konings, a Tanzanian form of A. jacobfreibergi.

Pseudotropheus demasoni, a recently described mbuna (A78170).

Of the probable 1.500 species of cichlids living in Lake Malawi, at present only about 400 have been scientifically described.

For this reason in the years to come many species will receive a valid name for the first time, or be transferred to different genera.

One example is *Maylandia,* which was first described as a subgeneric complex but has now been elevated to generic status.

left: This small piscivore, A29470, exported as Haplochromis sp. "Diamond", has not yet been identified. It is probably a Dimidiochromis species.

possible to publish pictures today of what remains to be discovered tomorrow, but these pages do, however, show a few recently discovered or little-known cichlids.

left: Protomelas „Spilonotus Tanzania"; a species in which males in courtship dress lose their dark midlateral stripes (A75120).

right: Labidochromis sp. „Mbamba"; only very recently imported for the first time, from Mbamba Bay (Tanzania) (A40075).

Further Informations
Bibliograpy, Glossary

BIBLIOGRAPHY:

AXELROD, H.R. (1974):
African Cichlids of Lakes Malawi
and Tanganyika. 2. Edition
T.F.H. Publications, Neptune City

DATZ-Sonderheft
Malawisee (1995),
Verlag Eugen Ulmer, Stuttgart

Deutsche Cichliden Gesellschaft (1995):
Cichliden. Festschrift zum
25jährigen Jubiläum der DCG

HERT, E. (1989):
The function of egg-spots in an
African mouth-brooding cichlid fish
(Anim. Behav., 37: 726-732)

HOLZBERG, S. (1978):
A field and laboratory study of the behaviour
and ecology of Pseudotropheus zebra
(BOULENGER), an endemic cichlid of Lake Malawi
(Pisces, Cichlidae). (Ztschr. Zool. Syst. Evol.
Forsch., 16: 171-187)

KONINGS, A. (1989):
Malawi Cichlids in their Natural Habitat
first edition
Verduijn Cichlids, Netherlands

KONINGS, A. (1991 onwards)
The Cichlids-Yearbook series
Cichlid Press

KONINGS, A. (1995):
Malawi Cichlids in their Natural Habitat, 2.ed.
Cichlid Press, Germany

MAYLAND, H.J. (1982):
Der Malawi-See und seine Fische
Landbuch-Verlag, Hannover

RIBBINK, A.J., MARSH, B.A., MARSH, A.C.,
RIBBINK, A.C., & B.J. SHARP (1983):
A preliminary survey of the cichlid fishes
of rocky habitats in Lake Malawi
South African Journal of Zoology, Vol.18, No.3

SCHRAML, E. (1998):
AQUALOG African Cichlids I: Malawi-Mbuna
Verlag A.C.S., Mörfelden-Walldorf

SPREINAT, A. (1994):
Malawisee-Cichliden aus Tansania
Unitext-Verlag, Bovenden

STAECK, W. (1974):
Cichliden – Verbreitung, Verhalten, Arten
Engelbert Pfriem Verlag, Wuppertal

STAECK, W. & LINKE, H. (1993):
African Cichlids II: Cichlids from Eastern Africa
Tetra-Verlag, Melle

STERBA, G. (1970):
Süßwasserfische aus aller Welt, Teil 2.
Verlag Neumann-Neudamm, Melsungen

TURNER, G. F. (1996):
Offshore Cichlids of Lake Malawi
Cichlid Press.

On literature about fish diseases see page 37!

GLOSSARY:

Gondwanaland: Hypothetical prehistoric southern continent (consisting of South America, Antarctica, Africa, India, and Australia), which originated from the original supercontinent Pangaea when the latter broke up as the result of plate tectonic movements.

Ichthyologist: A scientist who studies fishes.

Mbuna: Malawian fishermen's name for certain species, which has been adopted by scientists and aquarists, and applied to a large group of chiefly rock-dwelling cichlids.

Niche: A small, uniquely occupied/utilised, aspect (topographical and/or behavioural) (e.g. utilisation of a food source) of a biotope.

Ecological: Pertaining to the relationship between organisms and their environment, with emphasis on inter- and intra-specific relationships.

Ontogenesis: The development of an organism from fertilised oocyte to sexual maturity.

Plate tectonics: The theory pertaining to the movement of large, discrete, sections of the Earth's crust on the molten interior of the planet.

Population: The totality of the members of a species in a particular area.

Secondary freshwater fishes: Fishes whose ancestors originated in salt water and subsequently migrated into fresh.

Utaka: Malawian fishermen's name for a group of plankton-feeding intermediate-zone cichlids, now classified by scientists in the genus Copadichromis. The term is sometimes used more loosely by aquarists to include other planktonivores.

Index

Symbols

Continent of origin:

Simply check the letter in front of the code-number

A = Africa   **E** = Europe   **N** = North America

S = South + Central America   **X** = Asia + Australia

Age:

the last number of the code always stands
for the age of the fish in the photo:

1 = small   (baby, juvenile colouration)
2 = medium   (young fish / saleable size)
3 = large   (half-grown / good saleable size)
4 = XL   (fully grown / adult)
5 = XXL   (brooder)
6 = show   (show-fish)

Immediate origin:

W = wild
B = bred
Z = breeding-form
X = crossbreed

Size:

..cm = approximate size these fish can reach as
adults

Sex:

♂ male   ♀ female   ♂♀ pair

Temperature:

◁   18-22°C   (64 - 72°F)   (room temperature)
▷   22-25°C   (72 -77°F)   (tropical fish)
△   24-29°C   (75 - 85°F)   (Discus etc.)
▽   10-22°C   (50 - 72°F)   cold

pH-Value:

₿   pH 6,5 - 7,2 no special requirements (neutral)
↓P   pH 5,8 - 6,5 prefers soft, slightly acidic water
↑P   pH 7,5 - 8,5 prefers hard, alkaline water

Lighting:

○   bright, plenty of light / sun
◑   not too bright
◕   almost dark

Food:

☺   omnivorous / dry food, no special requirements
☺   food specialist, live food / frozen food
☻   predator, feed with live fish
☻   plant-eater, supplement with plant food

Swimming:

⊞   no special characteristics
⬆   in upper area / surface fish
⬇   in lower area / floor fish

Aquarium- set up:

▭   only floor and stones etc.
▨   stones / roots / crevices
▨   plant aquarium + stones / roots

Behaviour / reproduction:

♥   keep a pair or a trio
🐟   school fish, do not keep less than 10
🐟   egg-layer
🐟   livebearer / viviparous
🐟   mouthbrooder
🐟   cavebrooder
🐟   bubblenest-builder
●   algae-eater, glass-cleaner (roots + spinach)
◇   non aggressive fish, easy to keep (mixed aquarium)
⚠   difficult to keep, read specialist literature beforehand
🛑   warning, extremely difficult, for experienced specialists only
❶   the eggs need special care
§   protected species (WA), special license required ("CITES")

Minimum tank: capacity:

		Minimum tank:	capacity:
ss	super small	20 - 40 cm	5 - 20 l
s	small	40 - 80 cm	40 - 80 l
m	medium	60 - 100 cm	80 - 200 l
L	large	100 - 200 cm	200 - 400 l
XL	XL	200 - 400 cm	400 - 3000 l
XXL	XXL	over 400 cm	over 3000 l
			(show aquarium)

Inches

Centimeter

Key to the abbreviations of the scientific names

Example: **Belontia signata jonklaasi** Benl & Terofal, **1975**
       Genus   Species   Subspecies   Describer , Year of the publication

sp.:   **a species name is not yet available**

sp. aff.:   **similar species**
The species is not yet determined but it is very similar to the
one named in the following

cf.:   **in all probability this species**
The specimen shown or the respective population differs in
some minor details from the typical form, but these differences don't justify to place it into a species of its own.

Hybrid :   **Crossbreed**

ssp.:   **Subspecies**
Explanation: Some species inhabit an area of very wide range;
within this area, there are populations that differ significantly
from other populations in appearance, but seen genetically,
they belong nevertheless to the same species. Those populations get a third scientific name as geographical subspecies.
If a subspecies name has not yet been formally given, the
abbreviation spp. is added.

var. :   **Variation**
Explanation: Individual differences in colour combination,
which are not fixed in geographical areas, are so-called variations. They do not get a special scientific name.

Intergrade: **Mixed population of two subspecies**